STATES

NEVADA

A MyReportLinks.com Book

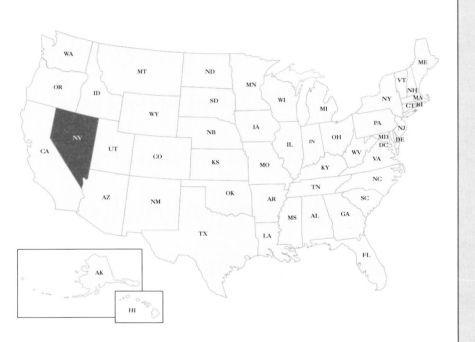

Stephen Feinstein

MyReportLinks.com Books

an imprint of
Enslow Publishers, Inc.
Box 398, 40 Industrial Road
Berkeley Heights, NJ 07922
USA

MyReportLinks.com Books, an imprint of Enslow Publishers, Inc.

Library of Congress Cataloging-in-Publication Data

Feinstein, Stephen.
   Nevada / Stephen Feinstein.
      p. cm. — (States)
     Summary: Discusses the land and climate, economy, government, and
history of the state of Nevada. Includes Internet links to Web sites.
Includes bibliographical references and index.
   ISBN 0-7660-5024-6
   1. Nevada—Juvenile literature. [1. Nevada.] I. Title. II.
Series: States (Series : Berkeley Heights, N.J.)
F841.3.F45 2002
979.3—dc21
                            2001008189

Printed in the United States of America

10 9 8 7 6 5 4 3 2 1

To Our Readers:
Through the purchase of this book, you and your library gain access to the Report Links that specifically back up this book.
The Publisher will provide access to the Report Links that back up this book and will keep these Report Links up to date on **www.myreportlinks.com** for three years from the book's first publication date.
We have done our best to make sure all Internet addresses in this book were active and appropriate when we went to press. However, the author and the Publisher have no control over, and assume no liability for, the material available on those Internet sites or on other Web sites they may link to.
The usage of the MyReportLinks.com Books Web site is subject to the terms and conditions stated on the Usage Policy Statement on **www.myreportlinks.com**.
In the future, a password may be required to access the Report Links that back up this book. The password is found on the bottom of page 4 of this book.
Any comments or suggestions can be sent by e-mail to comments@myreportlinks.com or to the address on the back cover.

Photo Credits: © 1995 Photodisc, p. 13; © 1999 Photodisc, pp. 26, 32; © Corel Corporation, pp. 3 (Constitution, Library of Congress), 10; Courtesy MyReportLinks.com Books, p. 4; Courtesy of American Memory, The Library of Congress, pp. 28, 38; Courtesy of Encyclopedia Britannica, p. 22; Courtesy of Exploring the Great Basin, p. 18; Courtesy of PBS, p. 41; Courtesy of PBS, The American Experience, p. 27; Courtesy of The Nevada Department of Cultural Affairs, p. 36; Courtesy of The U.S. Geological Survey, p. 20; Courtesy of The University of Nevada, Reno, p. 15; Courtesy of The University of Oregon, p. 16; Nevada Commission on Tourism, pp. 23, 29, 30, 34, 42, 44.

Cover Photo: Nevada Commission on Tourism

Cover Description: Lake Tahoe

Contents

MyReportLinks.com Books
Great Books, Great Links, Great for Research!

MyReportLinks.com Books present the information you need to learn about your report subject. In addition, they show you where to go on the Internet for more information. The pre-evaluated Report Links that back up this book are kept up to date on **www.myreportlinks.com**. With the purchase of a MyReportLinks.com Books title, you and your library gain access to the Report Links that specifically back up that book. The Report Links save hours of research time and link to dozens—even hundreds—of Web sites, source documents, and photos related to your report topic.

Please see "To Our Readers" on the Copyright page for important information about this book, the MyReportLinks.com Books Web site, and the Report Links that back up this book.

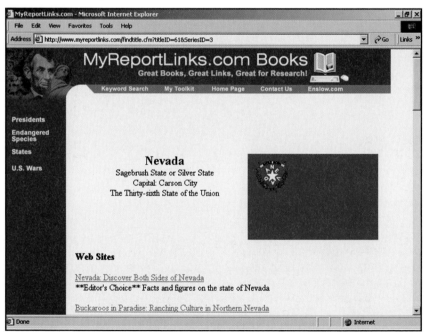

Access:

The Publisher will provide access to the Report Links that back up this book and will try to keep these Report Links up to date on our Web site for three years from the book's first publication date. Please enter **SNV6054** if asked for a password.

Report Links

The Internet sites described below can be accessed at
http://www.myreportlinks.com

EDITOR'S CHOICE

▶**Nevada: Discover Both Sides of Nevada**
At this Web site you will find facts and figures on the state of Nevada.
You will also find the biographies of some famous Nevadans, historical
information, and the text of the state constitution, among other things.

Link to this Internet site from http://www.myreportlinks.com

EDITOR'S CHOICE

▶**Buckaroos in Paradise: Ranching Culture in
Northern Nevada**
This Library of Congress site explores the ranching culture of northern
Nevada. Learn about the Buckaroos' way of life and the cowboy's creed.
You will also find a collection of films about haying.

Link to this Internet site from http://www.myreportlinks.com

EDITOR'S CHOICE

▶**A History of Native Nevadans Through Photography**
Learn about native Nevadans through a collection of photographs,
presented with a description of each image and historical information
providing insights into the lives and culture of the people of Nevada.

Link to this Internet site from http://www.myreportlinks.com

EDITOR'S CHOICE

▶**Hoover Dam**
This PBS Web site provides a comprehensive history of the Hoover
Dam. Included are a time line, maps, and information about the
people involved in the development of the dam, once considered
the eighth wonder of the world.

Link to this Internet site from http://www.myreportlinks.com

EDITOR'S CHOICE

▶**Re-Discover Nevada 2000: A Local Legacy**
America's Story from America's Library, a Library of Congress Web site,
provides a brief history of Nevada, including facts about the original
inhabitants and later settlers.

Link to this Internet site from http://www.myreportlinks.com

EDITOR'S CHOICE

▶**The Nevada Experience**
At this PBS Web site you will find a collection of Web sites relating to
Nevada. Some topics covered are Boulder City, German immigrants,
and the Great War.

Link to this Internet site from http://www.myreportlinks.com

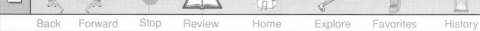

The Internet sites described below can be accessed at
http://www.myreportlinks.com

▶**Columbia Plateau Province: Snake River Plain**
The Snake River Plain, which stretches across Oregon, northern Nevada, southern Idaho, and ends at the Yellowstone Plateau in Wyoming, is explored in this Web site.

Link to this Internet site from http://www.myreportlinks.com

▶**Dat-So-La-Lee, Washoe Native American Woman**
At this Web site you will find a biography of Dat-So-La-Lee, a Washoe Indian woman who lived in Carson Valley and is well known for her basket weaving.

Link to this Internet site from http://www.myreportlinks.com

▶**Emma Nevada—An American Diva**
Take a virtual tour of Emma Nevada's life and work, from her birth in a California mining town to the opera stages of Europe. At this Web site you will find her biography, reviews of her performances, and photographs of the opera singer.

Link to this Internet site from http://www.myreportlinks.com

▶**Exploring the Great Basin!**
At this Web site you can take a virtual tour of the Great Basin. Here you can explore large areas of Nevada as well as parts of California, Idaho, Oregon, and Utah. The Great Basin includes the Great Salt Lake in Utah, and the Mojave Desert and Death Valley in California.

Link to this Internet site from http://www.myreportlinks.com

▶**Gold Rush**
At this PBS Web site you can learn all about the Gold Rush. In particular you will learn how many people traveled through Nevada on the Oregon Trail to get to California.

Link to this Internet site from http://www.myreportlinks.com

▶**History of the Newlands Irrigation Project**
The Newlands Irrigation Project was Nevada's first attempt to create a reliable water source. This Web site profiles the history of the project.

Link to this Internet site from http://www.myreportlinks.com

Report Links

The Internet sites described below can be accessed at
http://www.myreportlinks.com

▶**History of Virginia City, Nevada, and the Comstock Lode**
Take a virtual tour of the silver boomtown Virginia City, Nevada.
Learn about the Virginia and Truckee Railroad, Virginia City gas
lamps, and more.

Link to this Internet site from http://www.myreportlinks.com

▶**John C. Frémont: The Pathfinder**
At this Web site you will find a brief overview of John C. Frémont's
explorations and political life.

Link to this Internet site from http://www.myreportlinks.com

▶**Kit Carson**
At this Web site you will find a brief biography of Kit Carson. Here
you will learn how Carson served as John C. Frémont's guide while
exploring Oregon, California, the Great Basin, and the Central
Rocky Mountains.

Link to this Internet site from http://www.myreportlinks.com

▶**Mark Twain**
At this PBS Web site you can explore the life of Samuel Clemens,
better known as Mark Twain. Here you will learn about Twain's
life and adventures in Nevada and his job as a reporter for the
Territorial Enterprise.

Link to this Internet site from http://www.myreportlinks.com

▶**Native American History and Culture**
At this Web site you will find links to information about many
American Indian tribes, including those native to Nevada.

Link to this Internet site from http://www.myreportlinks.com

▶**Native Nevada Classroom**
At this site you will learn about native Nevadan Indians through a series
of Web-quests designed to teach students about the Washoe
tribe and other Nevada tribes.

Link to this Internet site from http://www.myreportlinks.com

		STOP						
Back	Forward	Stop	Review	Home	Explore	Favorites	History

Report Links

 The Internet sites described below can be accessed at
http://www.myreportlinks.com

▶ **Nevada**
At this Web site you will find a brief overview of the state of Nevada, including facts and figures about the state's climate, government, and much more.

Link to this Internet site from http://www.myreportlinks.com

▶ **Nevada**
America's Story from America's Library, a Library of Congress Web site, provides interesting facts about the state of Nevada. Here you will learn the origins of the state's name and much more!

Link to this Internet site from http://www.myreportlinks.com

▶ **Nevada Kids Page**
At the Nevada Kids Page Web site you will learn about Nevada's history, famous Nevadans, Nevada officials, and native Nevadans. You can also take a virtual tour of the state.

Link to this Internet site from http://www.myreportlinks.com

▶ **Nevada Native America On the WWW**
At this Web site you will find links to information about native Nevadans, including the Washoe Indians.

Link to this Internet site from http://www.myreportlinks.com

▶ **Race for the Super Bomb**
At this PBS Web site you can learn about nuclear testing sites (there are 935 in Nevada), top-secret bomb shelters, and a time line revealing the history of nuclear weapons.

Link to this Internet site from http://www.myreportlinks.com

▶ **Sarah Winnemucca**
This Web site offers a biography of Sarah Winnemucca, a Northern Paiute activist and lecturer and the author of "Life Among the Piutes: Their Wrongs and Claims," who defended the rights of her people.

Link to this Internet site from http://www.myreportlinks.com

Any comments? Contact us: **comments@myreportlinks.com**

Report Links

➤ The Internet sites described below can be accessed at
http://www.myreportlinks.com

▶**Smithsonian Magazine—Good Days at Black Rock**
At this Web site you will learn about some of the interesting events that
take place at Black Rock Desert such as the Burning Man Project, a
freewheeling arts festival.

Link to this Internet site from http://www.myreportlinks.com

▶**State of Nevada**
At the State of Nevada Web site you can learn about Nevada's history
and government. You can also explore the rich history of Nevada's
seventeen counties by navigating through the Nevada map.

Link to this Internet site from http://www.myreportlinks.com

▶**Stately Knowledge: Nevada**
At this Web site you will find facts and figures about Nevada as well as
links to almanacs, encyclopedias, and other useful Internet resources.

Link to this Internet site from http://www.myreportlinks.com

▶**The Story of Hoover Dam**
This site explains how the Colorado River was tamed by the
construction of the Hoover Dam. You will also find articles, essays,
images, maps, and oral histories relating to the history of Hoover Dam.

Link to this Internet site from http://www.myreportlinks.com

▶**Territorial Enterprise**
Learn about Virginia City's past by reading editorials written by Mark
Twain in the *Territorial Enterprise*, the local newspaper of the time.

Link to this Internet site from http://www.myreportlinks.com

▶**Valley of Fire State Park**
At this Web site you can view images of the Valley of Fire State Park,
near Lake Mead; learn about the park's history; and find out how it
got its name.

Link to this Internet site from http://www.myreportlinks.com

Nevada Facts

Capital
Carson City

Gained Statehood
October 31, 1864

Population
1,998,257*

Bird
Mountain bluebird

Trees
Bristlecone pine;
single-leaf piñon

Flower
Sagebrush

Mammal
Desert bighorn sheep

Reptile
Desert tortoise

Fish
Lahontan cutthroat trout

Fossil
Ichthyosaur

Gemstone
Black fire opal

Song
"Home Means Nevada"
(words and music by Bertha
Raffetto)

Motto
All for Our Country

Nicknames
Silver State, Sagebrush State

Flag
A silvery-white five-pointed star, representing Nevada's mineral wealth, appears in the upper-left corner against a blue background. On a yellow banner above the star are the words "Battle Born," pointing out that Nevada was admitted to the Union during the Civil War. A half-wreath of sagebrush, the state flower, appears below the star.[1]

Population reflects the 2000 census.

Chapter 1

The State of Nevada

Nevada, located in the southwestern part of the United States, is a place of amazing contrasts. Much of the state consists of vast, empty deserts. For this reason the government chose Nevada as the best state in which to carry out nuclear tests. On the other hand, the cities of Las Vegas in the south, and to a lesser extent Reno in the north, have experienced a population explosion in recent years. Indeed, Las Vegas is the fastest-growing city in the United States.

▶ The Silver State

For thousands of years, Nevada's only human inhabitants were scattered groups of American Indians. White settlers arrived in 1851, when Mormons established a small community near present-day Reno. During the next few years, thousands of people passed through Nevada. Most were prospectors headed for California, where the Gold Rush was in full swing. They could hardly wait to leave Nevada and its endless deserts. One prospector named Peter Decker warned, "[In Nevada] expect to find the worst desert you ever saw, and then find it worse than you expected."[1]

But then, in 1859, a prospector named James Finney discovered silver in the Nevada hills. The Comstock Lode was the richest source of silver ever found in the United States. It was named for the man who claimed to own the land. News of the discovery spread quickly, and fortune

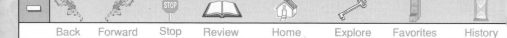

▲ *Virginia City is one of the towns that grew rapidly during the silver and gold boom of the mid-nineteenth century.*

seekers began to stream into Nevada. Among them were thousands of miners and prospectors from the gold fields of California.

Mining boomtowns sprang up practically overnight. In two years, Virginia City grew from a handful of miners in tents to a town of more than fifteen thousand people. When the silver boom eventually went bust, many thriving mining towns became ghost towns.

Although the Comstock Lode silver is gone, Nevada mines still produce gold, silver, copper, and other minerals, but on a much smaller scale. Virginia City is kept alive mainly by tourists. And most people flocking to the Silver State today are not interested in prospecting for silver or any other metal. They hope to strike it rich in a different way.

▶ Seekers of Fun and Fortune

Like a giant glittering magnet in the desert, Las Vegas attracts people from all over the world to its gambling, or "gaming," casinos and fabulous resort hotels. As many as 34 million visitors come to Las Vegas each year, and the number is growing. In a state with a history of boom-towns, Las Vegas must be the ultimate boomtown. The city's hotels are constantly being torn down and replaced by bigger and better pleasure palaces. Casinos along Las Vegas' famous Strip are open twenty-four hours a day, and offer a mind-boggling assortment of entertainment. Visitors are thrilled by lavish shows featuring dancers in spectacular costumes. Well-known acts from the world of showbiz perform in the glamorous nightclubs.

At any hour of the day or night, throngs of people crowd the casinos, hoping to make a quick fortune. Casino names—such as the Gold Spike, the Gold Coast, the Golden Nugget, Mahoney's Silver Nugget, and Silver

▲ *Millions of visitors flock to Las Vegas, one of the world's most famous resort cities.*

City—suggest the treasures to be won inside. But most people leave the casinos with less money than they brought with them. The slot machines, known as "one-armed bandits," continue to relieve visitors of their money at all hours of night and day. The "house," or casino, is the real winner. But most players are content to enjoy the fun and laughs.

Las Vegas is the biggest but certainly not the only gambling mecca in Nevada. Reno, Nevada's second-largest city, has some of the glitz of Las Vegas, but on a smaller scale. Small towns in the state have gambling casinos, too, and visitors can even find slot machines in supermarkets and Laundromats. Bright lights of small towns such as Winnemucca can been seen from 30 miles away. These are the flashing neon signs of just two or three casinos. Even past midnight, the casinos are full.

▶ Inspired by the Wild West

Over the years Nevada has been a source of inspiration for writers, artists, and musicians. Among them was the author Samuel Clemens (1835–1910), who wrote under the name Mark Twain. He was drawn to Virginia City in the early 1860s during the boomtown days of the Comstock Lode. In those days, Virginia City was a wild place. At one time there were more than forty saloons in the town. People were quick to settle arguments with guns, and gunfights on the streets of Virginia City were almost a daily occurrence. Twain observed such events with interest, and reported on them for the town newspaper, the *Territorial Enterprise.*

Twain also tried his hand at prospecting. One day, he saw glittering specks in the rock and thought he had discovered gold. Sadly, his discovery turned out to be mica,

Biography:

Sarah Winnemucca's birth coincided with the beginning of an era of dramatic historical changes for her people, changes in which she would play an important and often thankless role. She worked throughout her life to communicate between her people and the white people, to defend Paiute rights, and to create understanding.

"I was born somewhere near 1844, but am not sure of the precise time. I was a very small child when the first white people came into our country. They came like a lion, yes, like a roaring lion, and have continued so ever since, and I have never forgotten their first coming. My people were scattered at that time over nearly all the territory now known as Nevada. My grandfather was chief of the entire Piute nation, and was camped near Humboldt Lake, with a small portion of his tribe, when a party travelling eastward from California was seen coming. When the news was brought to my grandfather, he asked what they looked like? When told that they had hair on their faces, and were white, he jumped up and clasped his hands together and cried aloud--"My white brothers-- my long-looked for white brothers have come at last!" (Sarah Winnemucca, Life Among the Piutes).

Born into the Northern Paiute tribe in 1844, she was given the name Thocmetony, which means "shell flower":

▲ Sarah Winnemucca Hopkins, the daughter of a famous Paiute Indian chief, worked throughout her life to improve communication between the Paiute people and whites.

also called fool's gold. He described his disappointment in *Roughing It*, a book about his adventures in Nevada: "So vanished my dream. So melted my wealth away. . . . Moralizing, I observed then, that 'all that glitters is not gold.' "[2]

Another Nevadan writer of the time was Sarah Winnemucca Hopkins (1844?–91), the daughter of the famous Paiute Indian chief Winnemucca. Hopkins spoke out for American Indian rights and wrote several books about her people, among them *Life Among the Paiutes: Their Wrongs and Claims.*

In more recent years, the writer Walter Van Tilburg Clark (1909–71) lived and worked in Nevada. He wrote western novels, two of which, *The Ox-Bow Incident* and *Track of the Cat*, were made into Hollywood movies.

Some miners became extremely wealthy in Virginia City and other boomtowns of the time such as Gold Hill and Carson City. They built elegant mansions and opera houses. Opera singers from the East Coast made tours of the West. But one of the greatest and most popular opera stars was a Nevadan called Emma Wixom (1859–1946). As her fame grew, she changed her name to Emma Nevada, and went on to tour the country and Europe.

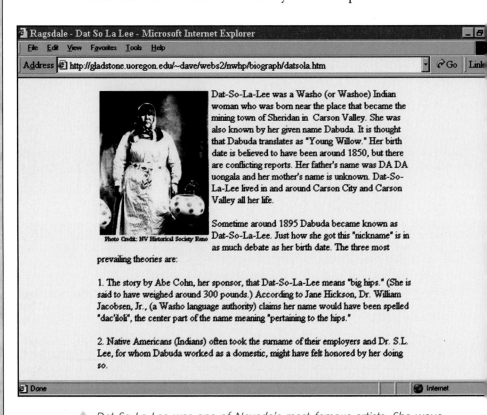

Ragsdale - Dat So La Lee - Microsoft Internet Explorer

File   Edit   View   Favorites   Tools   Help

Address http://gladstone.uoregon.edu/~dave/webs2/nwhp/biograph/datsola.htm   Go   Link

Dat-So-La-Lee was a Washo (or Washoe) Indian woman who was born near the place that became the mining town of Sheridan in Carson Valley. She was also known by her given name Dabuda. It is thought that Dabuda translates as "Young Willow." Her birth date is believed to have been around 1850, but there are conflicting reports. Her father's name was DA DA uongala and her mother's name is unknown. Dat-So-La-Lee lived in and around Carson City and Carson Valley all her life.

Photo Credit: NV Historical Society Reno

Sometime around 1895 Dabuda became known as Dat-So-La-Lee. Just how she got this "nickname" is in as much debate as her birth date. The three most prevailing theories are:

1. The story by Abe Cohn, her sponsor, that Dat-So-La-Lee means "big hips." (She is said to have weighed around 300 pounds.) According to Jane Hickson, Dr. William Jacobsen, Jr., (a Washo language authority) claims her name would have been spelled "dac'iloli", the center part of the name meaning "pertaining to the hips."

2. Native Americans (Indians) often took the surname of their employers and Dr. S.L. Lee, for whom Dabuda worked as a domestic, might have felt honored by her doing so.

Done   Internet

▲ Dat-So-La-Lee was one of Nevada's most famous artists. She wove beautiful baskets in the traditional Washo style, using only her teeth, fingernails, and a piece of sharp rock.

One of Nevada's most famous artists was the Washo Indian Dat-So-La-Lee (1829–1925), who lived in the Carson Valley not far from Virginia City. She made baskets in the traditional way of her people, using only her finger-nails, teeth, and a piece of sharp rock to weave the tough, dried willows in intricate patterns. She created more than 250 works of art in her life, sometimes spending several months on a single basket. Dat-So-La-Lee sold one of her finest baskets, called "Migration," for $10,000. Her work is on display at the Nevada State Museum in Carson City. The painter Robert Caples (1908–79) was inspired by the Indians of Nevada. He became famous for his murals depicting American Indian life.

Although the cowboy who rode the range in the Wild West is a vanishing breed today, true cowboys can still be found. They work on ranches scattered across the western states, including Nevada. Some of today's cowboys write poems about their lives. Every January, they come to Elko, Nevada, for the annual Cowboy Poetry Gathering. They recite their poems, some accompanying themselves on the guitar. By carrying on this tradition, the cowboys keep some of the spirit of the Wild West alive for themselves and their audience.

Chapter 2

Land and Climate

Nevada is the seventh-largest state, with an area of 110,567 square miles. It is bordered on the north by Oregon and Idaho, on the east by Utah, and on the southeast by Arizona. California borders Nevada on the west.

▶ Basin and Range Country

The Great Basin covers about 75 percent of Nevada. It mainly consists of wide, flat tracts of sagebrush-covered

Exploring the Great Basin! - Microsoft Internet Explorer

File   Edit   View   Favorites   Tools   Help

Address ⬚ http://www.goateye.com/dscrockett/wheeler.htm   ⬚ ⌀Go   Link

Ancient Bristlecone Pine in Great Basin National Park.

⬚ Done   🌐 Internet

▲ Bristlecone pines are ancient trees that can withstand harsh climates. The Great Basin bristlecone pine lives longer than any other tree.

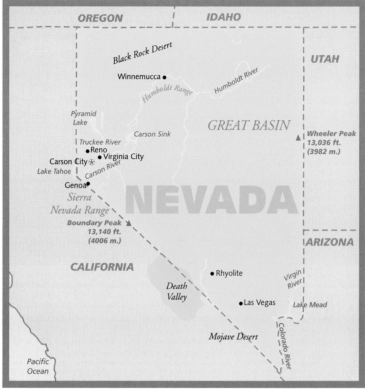

▲ A map of Nevada.

desert, at an average altitude of about 5,000 feet above sea level. The areas of desert or basin are in valleys between the more than two hundred mountain ranges that cross the state. The mountains rise as high as 5,000 feet above the basins, often reaching elevations of more than 10,000 feet. The mountains are often covered by forests of juniper and piñon pine, with other types of pine on the higher slopes.

Clinging to life at the very highest elevations, exposed to the harshest weather conditions, are bristlecone pines. These ancient trees, some of them more than four thousand years old, have been blasted by bitter winds into odd, twisted shapes. There is a forest of bristlecone pines at the

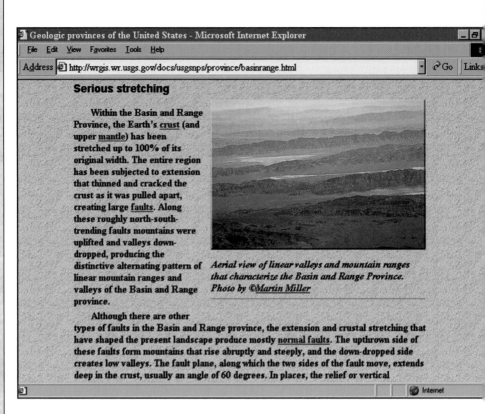

Serious stretching

Within the Basin and Range Province, the Earth's crust (and upper mantle) has been stretched up to 100% of its original width. The entire region has been subjected to extension that thinned and cracked the crust as it was pulled apart, creating large faults. Along these roughly north-south-trending faults mountains were uplifted and valleys down-dropped, producing the distinctive alternating pattern of linear mountain ranges and valleys of the Basin and Range province.

Aerial view of linear valleys and mountain ranges that characterize the Basin and Range Province. Photo by ©Martin Miller

Although there are other types of faults in the Basin and Range province, the extension and crustal stretching that have shaped the present landscape produce mostly normal faults. The upthrown side of these faults form mountains that rise abruptly and steeply, and the down-dropped side creates low valleys. The fault plane, along which the two sides of the fault move, extends deep in the crust, usually an angle of 60 degrees. In places, the relief or vertical

▲ *The breathtaking landscape of Nevada's Great Basin has inspired many writers, including John McPhee.*

Great Basin National Park near the town of Baker in the eastern part of the state. Various types of wild animals live there, including mountain lions (or cougars), deer, elk, and bighorn sheep.

Streams flow through some of the Great Basin's valleys. Cattle and sheep ranches can be found there. Cottonwood trees grow along the creeks. Elsewhere, wild horses known as mustangs, perhaps as many as thirty thousand of them, roam through the sagebrush. They are descended from horses that broke away from their owners. But except for some mining operations, the occasional ranch, and the few scattered towns, the Great Basin is a silent, empty land.

The writer John McPhee, impressed by the quiet stillness of Nevada's vast basin and range country, wrote, "Supreme over all is silence. Discounting the cry of the occasional bird, the wailing of a pack of coyotes, silence—a great spatial silence—is pure in the Basin and Range."[1]

South of the Great Basin is the Mojave Desert, which extends across the southern tip of the state. The city of Las Vegas is located here. The Mojave, at a lower elevation than the Great Basin Desert, has a hotter and drier climate. Creosote, yucca, and the Joshua tree are the native plants of the Mojave.

In the northeastern part of Nevada is an especially lonely region known as the Columbia Plateau. This flat highland is formed of hardened lava, the result of intense volcanic activity thousands of years ago. Rivers have cut many canyons in the plateau.

▶ The Jewel of the Sierra Nevada and Other Waterways

Straddling the Nevada-California border for about 400 miles is a magnificent snow-capped mountain range called the Sierra Nevada. "Sierra" means "mountain range" in Spanish and "Nevada," from which the state takes its name, means "covered by snow" in Spanish. Nevada's highest mountain, Boundary Peak, at an elevation of 13,140 feet, is in the Sierra. Scattered throughout the Sierra are beautiful mountain lakes.

Not far from Reno, Carson City, and Virginia City is Lake Tahoe, the crown jewel of the Sierra Nevada. The crystal-clear, deep blue lake is circled by the high peaks of the Sierra. Tahoe is right on the Nevada-California border, at an altitude of about 6,200 feet. It is the largest lake in the Sierra Nevada, and is believed to be one of the deepest

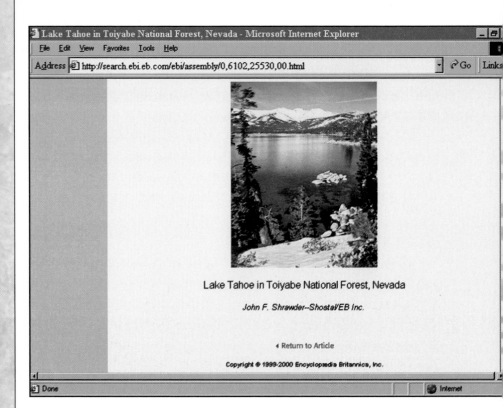

Lake Tahoe in Toiyabe National Forest, Nevada

John F. Shrawder–Shostal/EB Inc.

◄ Return to Article

Copyright © 1999-2000 Encyclopædia Britannica, Inc.

▲ *Lake Tahoe is a beautiful glacial lake that lies in the Sierra Nevada. It is one of the deepest lakes in the continental United States.*

lakes in the world. Mark Twain visited Lake Tahoe in 1861, shortly after arriving in Virginia City. He was dazzled by the beauty of Tahoe, writing, "the eye never tired of gazing, night or day, calm or storm; it suffered but one grief, and that was that it could not look always."[2]

Most of Nevada's rivers empty into lakes. The Truckee River flows from Lake Tahoe through Reno and into Pyramid Lake, so named because of its giant pyramid-shaped rock formation. Walker River also flows from the Sierra Nevada and ends in Walker Lake. Pyramid and Walker lakes are all that remain of the ancient Lake Lahontan, a giant lake that once covered about one tenth of Nevada. Over thousands of years, Lake Lahontan dried up, leaving only the two smaller lakes. A prehistoric species of fish, known as the cui-ui (kwee-wee), used to live in Lake Lahontan. Today, Pyramid Lake is the only place in the world in which cui-ui survive.

The Colorado River runs along Nevada's southeastern border with Arizona. In 1936, Hoover Dam was completed on the Colorado River, forming 245-square-mile Lake Mead, the largest man-made lake in the country.

▶ Freeze at Night, Fry at Noon

Nevada is the driest of the fifty states, with an average of only nine inches of rain a year. Las Vegas gets even less, only about four inches a year, while as much as twenty-five inches fall in the Sierra Nevada. The Sierra is responsible for the extreme dryness of Nevada's Great Basin. Winter storms blowing in from the Pacific drop most of their rain or snow on the western side of the mountains, before reaching the Great Basin. This is called the rainshadow effect of the Sierra.

The harsh weather conditions ▶ of the Great Basin are created by the Sierra Nevada.

Summer, especially in the southern part of the state, is known as "monsoon" season. Strong thunderstorms moving up from the south can dump more rain in an hour than many places receive in half a year. Such storms bring with them the danger of flash floods.

In the northern part of the state, winters are cold and much of the precipitation falls as snow, especially in the mountains. Many locations record subzero temperatures, which explains why 80 percent of Nevada's population lives in the south. Nevada's record low temperature of −50°F occurred at San Jacinto on January 8, 1937. But in the south, the winters are mild and pleasant. The average wintertime temperature in Las Vegas is 45°F. The afternoons are often warm and sunny with a temperature in the mid 60s. At night, however, the temperature can fall to the 20s. In the summer, it is hot and hotter, depending on how far south you happen to be. Las Vegas, in the far south, has long, hot summers, with the temperature often reaching 110 to 115°F. The highest temperature ever recorded in Nevada was 125°F at Laughlin, near Las Vegas, on June 29, 1994.

As is characteristic of a desert land far from any major body of water, the daily temperature ranges are extreme. On clear days the temperature often reaches 100°F or higher. But as soon as the sun goes down, the temperature drops rapidly, and during the night can fall to as low as 32°F.

Economy

Nevada's economy has prospered in recent years. This is due primarily to the growth of tourist-related businesses, which employ about 35 percent of the workforce. The increasing number of tourists has led to the need for more and more service workers to cater to the visitors' needs. This in turn has led to the rapid growth of Nevada's population. Indeed, Nevada has been the nation's fastest-growing state since 1960. The population grew 66 percent from 1990 to 2000, the largest increase in the United States.[1] The boom in tourism has led that industry to replace silver mining as the most important business in the state. Tourism, manufacturing, agriculture, and even the mining that still takes place in Nevada all require an essential resource—water. And water is a scarce commodity in a desert environment.

▶ Nevada's Most Valuable Resource

Most of Nevada's water comes from rivers. The Newlands Irrigation Project, completed in 1907, was Nevada's first major attempt to provide a reliable source of water. The project consisted of a system of dams built on the Truckee and Carson rivers near Reno. The Newlands Project allowed farms and ranches to flourish in the Carson Valley. In 1936, the Hoover Dam was built on the Colorado River along Nevada's southeastern border with Arizona. It was the world's largest dam at the time, and some called it the eighth wonder of the world. It provided enough water

▲ *The Colorado River is one of the major rivers in the United States. When the Hoover Dam was completed, in 1936, the Colorado River became a source of water and hydroelectric power for remote parts of Nevada.*

and hydroelectric power to make possible the rapid growth of nearby Las Vegas.

A major portion of Nevada's water, about 33 percent, comes from large pools of water beneath the ground, known as aquifers. It has taken thousands of years for this underground supply of water to form. Nevadans in many parts of the state tap into the aquifers by drilling wells. Over the years, the groundwater has been used for agriculture and manufacturing, as well as for homes. But Nevadans wonder how long this source of water will last. With each passing year, the water level in the aquifers gets lower. To prevent the groundwater from drying up, Nevadans will need to find ways to conserve water.

▶ Gold and Silver, Cattle and Sheep

Although the silver-mining boom in the days of the Comstock Lode is a distant memory, mining is still important in Nevada. It is the state's number two industry after tourism. Indeed, Nevada is the nation's largest producer of silver and gold. However, less than two percent of Nevada's workforce are employed in mining.

Even fewer Nevadans are employed in agriculture—less than one percent of the state's workforce. Still, there are about three thousand farms, mostly small ones, scattered about the state. The main products are wheat, hay, potatoes, and barley. About 1,700 ranches, mainly in the northeastern part of the state, raise cattle and sheep. Many ranchers are descendants of Basques from Spain, who settled in northern Nevada in the 1880s and herded sheep.

Manufacturing is a growing part of Nevada's economy today, employing about 5 percent of the state's workforce.

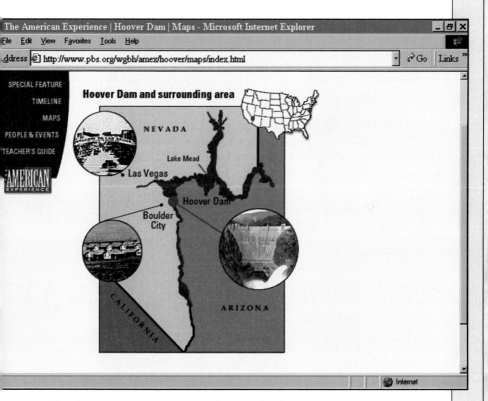

The American Experience | Hoover Dam | Maps - Microsoft Internet Explorer

File   Edit   View   Favorites   Tools   Help

Address http://www.pbs.org/wgbh/amex/hoover/maps/index.html   Go   Links

SPECIAL FEATURE
TIMELINE
MAPS
PEOPLE & EVENTS
TEACHER'S GUIDE
AMERICAN
EXPERIENCE

Hoover Dam and surrounding area

NEVADA

Lake Mead

Las Vegas

Hoover Dam

Boulder City

CALIFORNIA

ARIZONA

▲ The Hoover Dam is a national historic landmark.

The main industries are publishing and printing, computers, electrical equipment, and metal products.

▶ Millions and Millions of Tourists

Approximately 40 million people visit Nevada each year. Las Vegas, the world's most famous resort city, receives about 34 million visitors a year, while Reno receives about 5 million. Most come mainly to have a good time, although some come for business conventions or conferences. But Nevada has much more to offer beyond the glittering hotels and gaming casinos where visitors hope to hit the jackpot. Many tourists seek out the variety of

▲ Ranchers rope calves for spring branding to identify a ranch's herd.

activities and sightseeing experiences available elsewhere in the Silver State.

Many visitors enjoy golf and there are many golf courses to choose from. A more unusual experience is to go for a ride in a hot-air balloon over the Las Vegas Valley. Close to Las Vegas are Hoover Dam and Lake Mead, where visitors can go swimming, boating, or waterskiing. Also near Las Vegas is the Valley of Fire State Park, with its spectacular red rocks formed into strange shapes by windblown sand. Within a two-hour drive from Las Vegas is the ghost town of Rhyolite, which once had a population of twelve thousand. Nearby is the Nevada portion of Death Valley National Park (most of which lies across the border in California). Further north near Reno, the mountains just above Lake Tahoe offer ideal ski slopes in the wintertime. Also near Reno is Virginia City, the major boomtown of the Comstock Lode.

Many tourists are attracted to the tiny town of Rachel. Strange things are said to happen at

Las Vegas is renowned for its bustling casinos, lavish hotels, and re-creations of famous landmarks. Two of these, the Statue of Liberty and the Empire State Building, tower above the New York Hotel in Las Vegas.

▲ *UFO sightings have been reported along Nevada's Extraterrestrial Highway.*

nearby Area 51, a secret U.S. Air Force base. Trespassing is strictly forbidden at Area 51, where the Air Force is known to test experimental aircraft. But over the years, there have been wild rumors about UFOs. Some of the local towns-people claim not only to have seen UFOs, but to have been visited by them. Some even say that aliens from another world are being held captive at the base. So tourists park their cars alongside U.S. Highway 375 near the Air Force base. They stand around in the dark for hours, staring at the night sky with their telescopes or binoculars, hoping to see a UFO. Whether or not there is any truth to the rumors, the Nevada Department of Transportation put up road signs on Highway 375, designating a 92-mile stretch of the road "Extraterrestrial Highway."

Government

On October 31, 1864, Nevada became the thirty-sixth state to enter the Union. Because the Civil War was still raging at the time, the words "Battle Born" appear on the Nevada state flag. Nevada and West Virginia were the only states admitted to the Union during the Civil War.

▶ Nevada's Constitution

Nevada's constitution dates back to 1864. The federal government required that a territory applying for admission to the Union as a state had to have its constitution on file in Washington, D.C. Nevadans feared that it would take too long to send the constitution to Washington by train. So they sent the entire document, word for word, by telegraph.

Nevada's constitution outlines the structure of the state government and spells out the powers of its various branches and departments. Nevada is still governed by its constitution of 1864, although there have been many changes to it since then. Each amendment was approved by a majority of Nevada's voters. All Nevadans over the age of eighteen are eligible to vote, as long as they have lived in the state for more than thirty days.

▶ The Structure of Nevada's Government

Using the federal government as a model, the Nevada Constitution divides the state government into three branches—executive, legislative, and judicial. Just as in the

federal government, there is a separation of powers. The executive branch carries out the laws, the legislative branch creates the laws, and the judicial branch interprets the laws. The chief executive is the governor, who is elected by the voters to a four-year term. The governor, who is responsible for seeing that the laws of the state are enforced, can serve a maximum of two terms. There are five other elected officials in the executive branch: the lieutenant governor, attorney general, secretary of state, controller, and treasurer. Each of these officials reports to the governor, and can serve a maximum of two four-year terms.

The legislative branch of Nevada's government consists of a twenty-one-member senate and a forty-two-member assembly. Senators are elected by the voters to a four-year term of office. Assembly members are elected to a two-year term. The main job of the legislators is to propose new laws. When both houses approve a proposal, it is sent to the governor to be signed into law. If the governor vetoes the proposed new law,

▲ The State Capitol Building in Carson City.

both houses of the legislature can override the veto with a two-thirds vote.

The judicial branch of Nevada's government consists of the state supreme court with a chief justice and four associate judges, the district courts—Nevada's basic trial courts—and the municipal courts. There is no court of appeals. To be appealed, cases have to go directly from the municipal or district courts to the state supreme court.

Nevada's state government needs billions of dollars a year in order to function. Still, Nevada has no state income tax, nor is there a corporate tax on businesses. Nevada does have a 6.5 percent sales tax, but most of the money to run the government comes from taxes paid by gambling casinos. Thanks to government revenue raised from the casinos, Nevada's public schools and libraries are among the finest in the nation.

The Federal Government in Nevada

Numerous federal agencies are involved in managing the 85 percent of Nevada's land that is owned by the federal government. These include the Forest Service, Fish and Wildlife Service, National Park Service, and Bureau of Land Management. The U.S. Navy, Army, and Air Force are also involved in Nevada. Fighter planes from the huge Nellis Air Force Base are used in training exercises all year round. And the famous Navy Fighter Weapons School at Fallon, known as "Top Gun," provides flight and air-combat classes to fighter pilot trainees.

Chapter 5

History

There was once a time when wild animals such as the woolly mammoth and mastodon, relatives of the elephant, were the only inhabitants of the vast land that is now Nevada. Human beings had not yet set foot on the North American continent. It was the last Ice Age, and much of North America was buried under thick sheets of ice. Then, sometime between 20,000 and 40,000 years ago, groups of nomadic hunters began migrating from Asia to North America. Following herds of animals, they wandered across a land bridge that then connected Alaska and Siberia. By about 11,000 B.C., the first people entered Nevada.

▶ The Earliest Nevadans

Archaeologists refer to the first people in Nevada, the ancestors of American Indians, as Paleo-Indians. They lived a nomadic lifestyle. They lived in caves

◀ *The largest ichthyosaur fossils in the world can be found at Nevada's Berlin-Ichthyosaur State Park.*

and rock shelters, and hunted, fished, and gathered fruits, nuts, and berries. Human bones and spear points found in caves near Lovelock, Las Vegas, and other places in the state are believed to be more than eleven thousand years old. Also found in the caves were items such as darts, fishhooks, stone tools, baskets, and shell jewelry.

Over the course of thousands of years, Nevada's Paleo-Indians had to adjust to changing conditions. During the early centuries, as the Ice Age was ending, the glaciers melted. Water was plentiful, and plant and animal life were abundant. Eventually, however, the climate became drier. Giant Lake Lahontan shrank and disappeared except for two much smaller lakes. Many other rivers and lakes dried up also. Nevada was changing into a desert environment.

By about A.D. 200, native people known as the "Anasazi," a Navajo word meaning "Ancient Ones," were developing a farming culture in present-day New Mexico, Arizona, and the southern part of Nevada. The Indians of the early Anasazi period, known as the Basket Makers, were skilled at making tightly woven baskets of dried grasses. The Anasazi grew corn, beans, and squash in irrigated fields, and they made beautiful brightly painted pottery. By about A.D. 500, they began building apartment houses out of rock or mud bricks. Known as pueblos, some of the buildings had more than a hundred rooms. Anasazi of this later period are known as Pueblo Indians. The Anasazi civilization flourished for nearly a thousand years. Then, around A.D. 1300, the Anasazi disappeared. No one knows why, but a severe drought lasting many years is a likely reason. In the southeastern corner of Nevada are the ruins of an Anasazi city known as Pueblo Grande de Nevada.

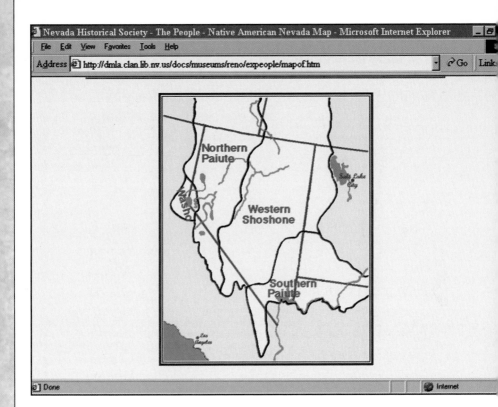

Nevada Historical Society - The People - Native American Nevada Map - Microsoft Internet Explorer

File   Edit   View   Favorites   Tools   Help

Address http://dmla.clan.lib.nv.us/docs/museums/reno/expeople/mapof.htm   Go   Links

Northern
Paiute

Salt Lake
City

Washo

Western
Shoshone

Southern
Paiute

Los
Angeles

Done   Internet

This map shows the parts of Nevada that various American Indian tribes occupied.

At about the time the Anasazi civilization collapsed, other groups of American Indians were moving into what is now Nevada. The Southern Paiute occupied the land of the Anasazi, while the Northern Paiute lived in the high basin and mountain range country in the north. The Washo Indians lived in the west, in the vicinity of Lake Tahoe in the Sierra Nevada. The Shoshone people lived in the east. These new groups of American Indians were peaceful, nomadic hunters. Most of their energy was devoted to the challenge of finding enough to eat. Each group adapted well to the difficult desert environment. For more than six hundred years, nothing would happen to upset the Indians' way of life. Then the Europeans arrived.

Explorers, Trappers, Settlers, and Miners

In the late 1500s, Spaniards from Mexico explored the lands that are now the American Southwest. They claimed vast territories in the name of Spain. They built the town of Santa Fe, New Mexico, in 1610. Other settlements in New Mexico, Arizona, and California followed. In 1776, a Spanish priest named Francisco Garcés became the first white man to enter what is now Nevada. He was searching for a route between the Spanish missions in New Mexico and those along the coast of California. Although Garcés led his expedition across the southern tip of Nevada, the Spaniards did not establish any settlements there.

In 1821, Mexico won its independence from Spain. Nevada and the other lands that would one day become American states now belonged to Mexico. In the next few years, American fur trappers entered Nevada in search of beaver and fox pelts. In 1826, Jedediah Smith led a party of trappers through various parts of Nevada. The men suffered severe hardships in Nevada's deserts. In 1828, Peter Skene Ogden and a group of trappers hunted beaver along the Humboldt River. The following year Ogden became the first white man to cross the Great Basin from north to south.

The first tragic encounter in Nevada between white men and Indians occurred in 1833. That year, a mountain man named Joseph Walker led a group of fifty fur trappers along the Humboldt River. When they came across a band of Northern Paiute Indians, a fight broke out. Walker and his men fired at the Indians, who had never seen guns before. About forty of the Paiute were killed.

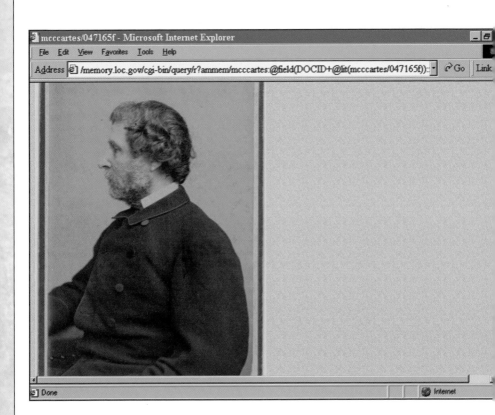

John C. Frémont is sometimes called "The Pathfinder," because he explored much of the area between the Rocky Mountains and the Pacific Ocean during the mid-nineteenth century. He also helped to produce the first scientific map of the western United States.

In 1843, John C. Frémont, a U.S. Army lieutenant, was assigned the task of exploring and mapping what is now Nevada. With Kit Carson as his guide, he crossed northern Nevada. Frémont noticed that the rivers either emptied into lakes or dried up in the desert, instead of flowing to the sea. So he named the region the Great Basin. He also gave the name Pyramid Lake to the lake with the pyramid-shaped rock formation.

During the 1840s, pioneer families in covered wagons began crossing Nevada's Great Basin on their way from

Missouri to a new life in California. The Bidwell-Bartleson party in 1841 was the first such group. Then in 1848, gold was discovered at Sutter's Mill in California and the Gold Rush began. Thousands of prospectors headed west across Nevada's deserts on their way to California. Also in 1848, the United States ended a three-year war with Mexico and gained the vast territory that would become the southwestern United States, including Nevada. This provided a further incentive for settlement of the West. The Mormons built a log fort near present-day Reno in 1851. Settlers established the community of Mormon Station around the fort. The name was later changed to Genoa. Meanwhile, in southern Nevada, Mormon missionaries built a stockade at a place called Las Vegas, which means "The Meadows" in Spanish.

During the 1850s, more families settled in the Carson River Valley near Genoa and began to farm the land. Nevada at that time was part of the Utah Territory, whose first governor was Brigham Young. In 1855, Chief Winnemucca of the Northern Paiute negotiated a Treaty of Friendship with the whites. But peace lasted only five years.

In 1859, after word got out about the silver discovery of the Comstock Lode, thousands upon thousands of prospectors flocked to Nevada. Virginia City and many other mining boomtowns sprang up. The huge influx of white men eventually led to conflict with the American Indians of the area. The newcomers were often disrespectful. They trespassed on Indian hunting grounds, killing animals and chopping down trees. In 1860, white traders kidnapped several Indian women. The Paiute retaliated by killing the traders. When an army of a hundred whites set off to attack the Indians, the Indians ambushed them near Pyramid Lake, killing seventy-six whites. Later, a larger

force of more than 550 whites attacked the Paiute, killing about 160 Indians. In the end, Chief Winnemucca had to agree to live with his people on a reservation at Pyramid Lake.

The silver boom was in full swing throughout the 1860s. The Pony Express began service in 1860. Pony riders delivered the mail from St. Louis, Missouri, to Sacramento, California, and to all points along the route, which crossed Nevada's Great Basin. It took a team of riders only ten days to travel 2,000 miles. In 1861, the year the Civil War began in the United States, the U.S. government created the Nevada Territory. President Abraham Lincoln wanted access to Nevada's silver to pay for the war. In 1864, Nevada, the "battle born" state, was admitted to the Union.

In 1869, the transcontinental railroad was completed. The railroad brought more settlers to Nevada. Then, during the 1870s, the silver boom came to an end. The federal government decided to place more value on gold for coins, and to pay less for silver. Also, the Comstock Lode silver had mostly been mined already. Although there would be another mining boom in another part of Nevada in the early 1900s, mining would never again be the main driver of the state's economy.

▶ The World's Biggest Boomtown

During the days of the Comstock Lode silver boom, gambling was legal in Nevada's mining towns. That ended when the boom ended. In 1931, during the Great Depression, Nevada's state legislature legalized gambling again. This made the state very attractive to tourists. Movie stars and other wealthy people had already begun flocking to Reno. The town was known as a place where a couple

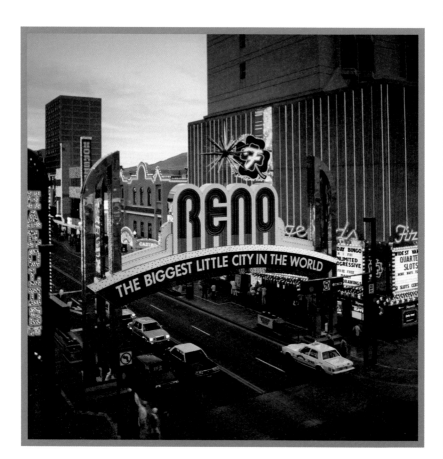

▲ Known as the "Biggest Little City in the World," Reno became a popular tourist destination in the early 1930s.

could get married or divorced quickly and easily. Reno called itself "the Biggest Little City in the World." In the mid-1930s, Harold Smith opened Harold's Club, a gambling casino featuring slot machines and card games. Prosperity filled the air as new hotels were built in Reno to cater to the hordes of visitors.

Meanwhile, a sleepy little town in southern Nevada, called Las Vegas, was beginning to wake up. Las Vegas was founded in 1905, when a railroad connecting Salt Lake City and Los Angeles was completed. The tiny town at first

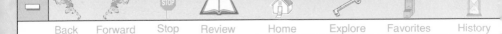

▲ *The construction of the Hoover Dam, pictured here, brought dramatic growth to Las Vegas during the Great Depression.*

was nothing more than a whistle-stop along the railroad. The 1930s brought dramatic growth to Las Vegas. While most of the nation suffered through the Depression, about five thousand workers arrived in Las Vegas in 1930 to build the gigantic Hoover Dam. The project took five years to complete. Las Vegas now had a new major tourist attraction—Lake Mead. Hotels and gambling casinos were built. More and more visitors arrived.

During the late 1930s, organized crime entered Las Vegas. Benjamin "Bugsy" Siegel, an associate of Meyer

Lansky and other well-known gangsters, began buying shares in downtown casinos. In the early 1940s, during World War II, thousands of military personnel were trained at nearby Nellis Air Force Base. By the end of the war, Las Vegas's population had grown to 17,000. Little Las Vegas was on its way to transforming itself into the world's biggest boomtown.

In 1946, Siegel built the Flamingo Hotel and gambling casino at a cost of five million dollars, a huge sum of money at the time. Unfortunately, shortly after the hotel opened, Bugsy was murdered by his associates, who continued to build and manage Las Vegas hotels and casinos for the next twenty years. By the late 1960s, Nevada's government was taking strong action against organized crime. Billionaire Howard Hughes bought several of the major hotels and casinos in Las Vegas. The city would no longer allow organized crime to run its major industry. In recent years, there has been a trend to turn Las Vegas into a vacation destination for the whole family.

The Atomic Age

In 1950 the federal government was looking for a place to conduct tests of nuclear bombs. And they found the perfect place—a 1,350-square-mile area of unpopulated desert in southern Nevada. From 1951 to 1962, America's nuclear scientists and military planners detonated 126 atomic bombs in the atmosphere and 925 below the ground. The fireballs from the nuclear blast could be seen 300 miles away in Reno, and the ground shook in Las Vegas, which was less than 100 miles from ground zero.

Atomic bomb tests took place about once a month, and almost became routine for many Nevadans. Most people seemed unaware that there might be any danger of

▲ *Since the end of the atomic boom that occurred after World War II, Nevada has been faced with the challenge of removing massive amounts of nuclear waste. In recent years, Nevadans have become more environmentally conscious and protective of their state's wildlife.*

exposure to radiation. Many even enjoyed the spectacle, and rooftop parties were organized in Las Vegas in order to view the event. Local businesses sold "atom" burgers and "nuclear" gasoline. But there were people who had a completely different reaction, such as the seventeen-year-old soldier who said, "That cloud was like a big ball of fire with black smoke and some red inside, big, monstrous, almost sickening . . . It left me really sad, real apprehensive about life . . . That explosion told me I was part of the most evil thing I have ever seen in my life."[1]

Many years have gone by since the last nuclear weapon was detonated in Nevada. But today, once again, the federal government has plans for Nevada involving the nuclear industry. This time, the state is being asked to accept the nation's radioactive waste for storage in a disposal site at Yucca Mountain, 100 miles northwest of

Las Vegas. The Department of Energy plans to deposit the radioactive waste 1,000 feet below the surface.

Many Nevadans today are concerned about the environment. They oppose storing nuclear waste at Yucca Mountain because they believe many safety issues have not been resolved. Nevada politicians including U.S. Senator Richard Bryan have managed to delay the storage plan until the year 2010. As Nevada continues to grow in the twenty-first century, Nevadans will also have to make wise decisions about other environmental issues, such as the best way to manage the state's water resources. With good planning, Nevada will continue to be a beautiful and exciting place for both residents and visitors.

Nevada Facts

1. *USA State Symbols, Flags & Facts,* CD-ROM, Canada: Robesus, Inc., 2001.

Chapter 1. The State of Nevada

1. Peter Decker as quoted by Patricia Nelson Limerick, "The Significance of Deserts in American History," *Desert Passages,* n.d., <http://carbon.cudenver.edu/stc-link/weblink/water/materials/limerick-swd.html> (March 19, 2002).

2. Mark Twain, *Roughing It,* as quoted in "Appearances," *Twainquotes.com,* n.d., <http://www.twainquotes.com/Appearances.html> (March 20, 2002).

Chapter 2. Land and Climate

1. John McPhee, *Basin and Range* (New York: Farrar, Straus, Giroux, 1980), p. 46.

2. Mark Twain, as quoted in Deke Castleman, *Moon Handbooks: Nevada* (Emeryville, Calif.: Avalon Travel Publications, 2001), p. 172.

Chapter 3. Economy

1. "Ranking Tables for States," *Census 2000,* April 2, 2001, <http://www.census.gov/population/cen2000/phc-t2/tab01.txt> (June 5, 2001).

Chapter 5. History

1. Carole Gallagher, quoting a soldier in *American Ground Zero: The Secret Nuclear War,* as quoted in Deke Castleman, *Moon Handbooks: Nevada* (Emeryville, Calif.: Avalon Travel Publications, 2001), p. 22.

Further Reading

Durham, Michael S. *The Smithsonian Guide to Historic America: The Desert States.* New York: Stewart, Tabori & Chang, Inc., 1990.

Lynch, Don, David Thompson, and James H. Bean, ed. *Battle Born Nevada: People History Stories.* Second ed. Carson City, Nev.: Grace Dangberg Foundation, Inc., 1998.

Melton, Rollan. *Nevadans.* Reno: University of Nevada Press, 1988.

Purdue, Matt. *Adventure Guide to Nevada.* Edison, N.J.: Hunter Publishing, Inc. 1999.

Sirvaitis, Karen. *Nevada.* Minneapolis, Minn.: Lerner Publications, 1992.

Stefoff, Rebecca. *Nevada.* Tarrytown, N.Y.: Marshall Cavendish Corporation, 2001.

Stein, R. Conrad. *Nevada.* Second ed. Danbury, Conn.: Children's Press, 2000.

Stratton, David. *Las Vegas and Beyond.* Berkeley, Calif.: Ulysses Press, 1993.

Thompson, David and Donald Dickerson, ed. *Nevada: A History of Changes.* Fourth ed. Carson City, Nev.: Grace Dangberg Foundation, Inc., 1986.

White, Michael C. *Nevada Wilderness Areas and Great Basin National Park.* Berkeley, Calif.: Wilderness Press, 1997.

Index